Pippa and Pop

3 Letters and Numbers Workbook

T0268730

○ **Trace.**

Review the alphabet. Then the children identify and trace the letters with colored pencils.

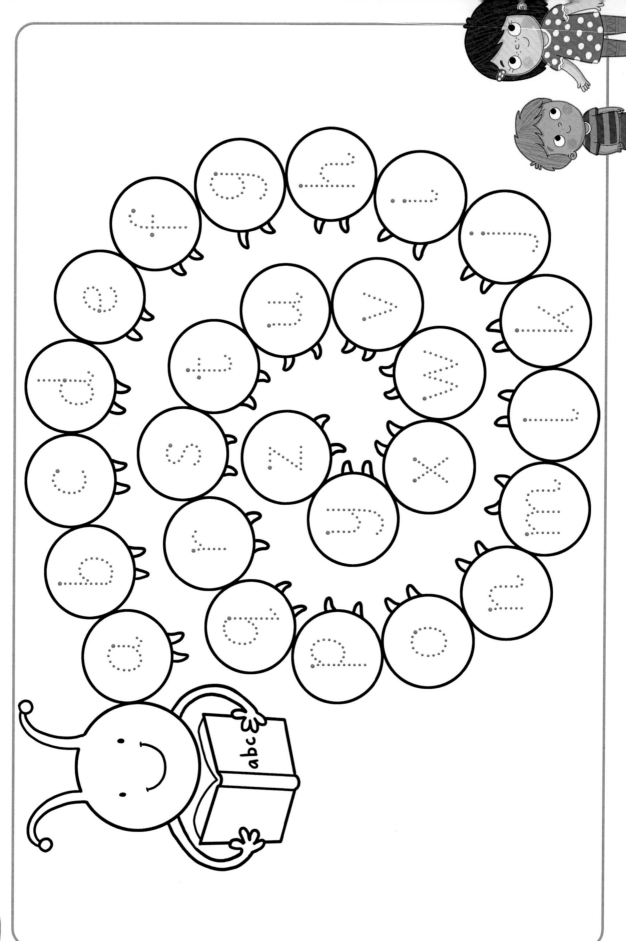

Match. Color.

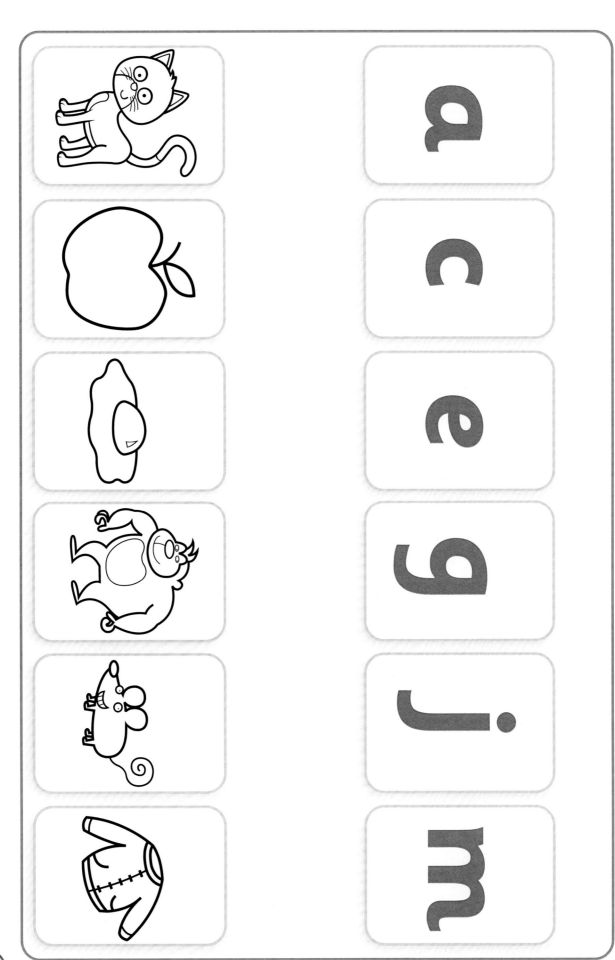

a c e g j m

Review the alphabet. Then the children look at the letters and draw a line to match them with the corresponding pictures. Finally, they color the pictures freely.

The children circle the letter each picture starts with. Then they color in the pictures freely.

n	j	l
		f
p	t	q
		r
w	x	y
		v
b	s	k
		z

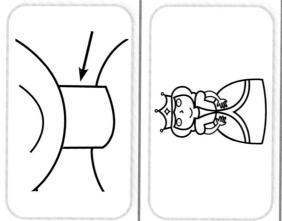

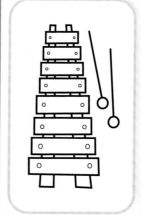

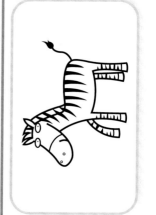

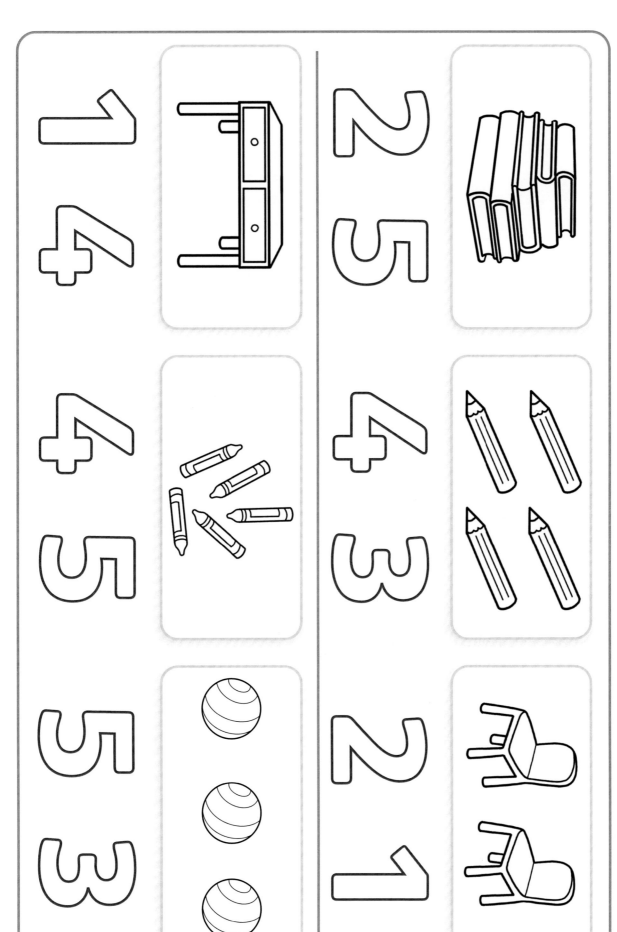

Count. ○ Circle. ✎ Color.

2 5

4 3

2 1

1 4

4 5

5 3

Review the numbers from 1 to 5. Then the children count the objects in each box and circle the corresponding number. Finally, they color the objects and numbers freely.

⬭ Trace. ✋ Count. ✏ Color.

Review the numbers from 1 to 10. Then the children point to the number **9**, trace it and count and color nine crayons. Repeat the procedure for the remaining numbers and items.

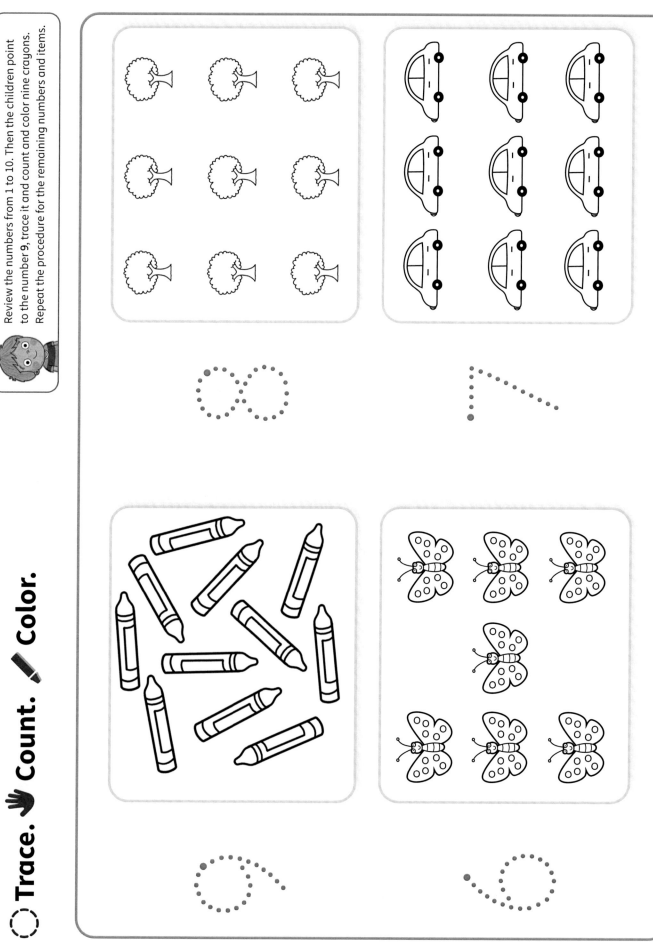

✏ Write. 🖍 Color.

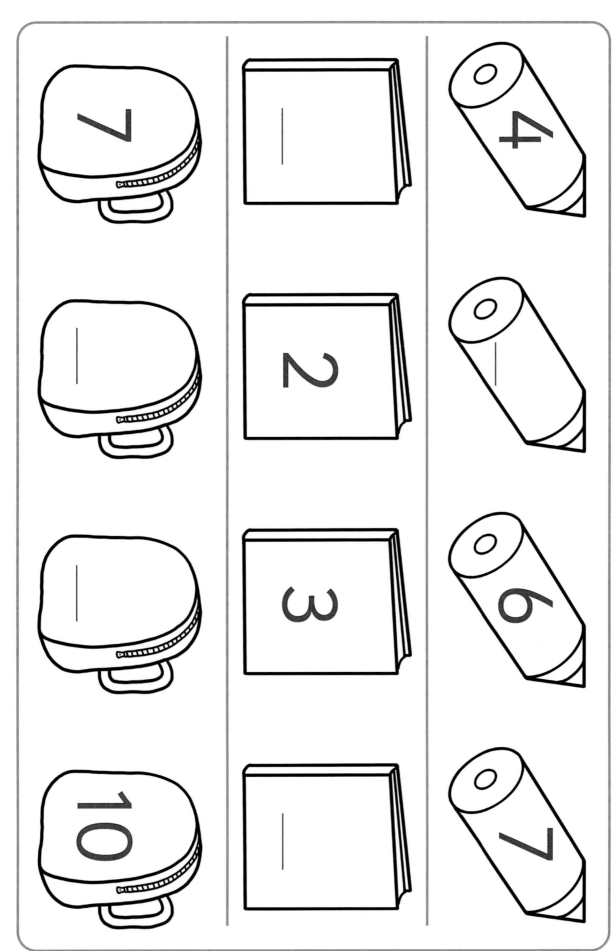

Review the numbers from 1 to 10. Then the children look at the first series of numbers and write the missing number. Repeat the procedure for the remaining series. Finally, they color the pictures freely.

○ Trace. ✏ Color.

The children identify the daily activities.
Then they trace the words with colored pencils.
Finally, the children color the pictures freely.

brush my teeth

get dressed

have breakfast

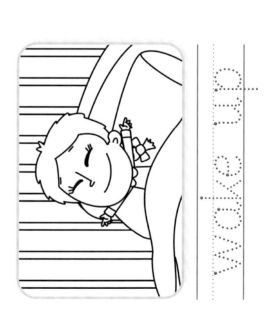

wake up

I wash my face.

I brush my hair.

I love breakfast.

The children trace the words with colored pencils. Then they color the corresponding picture.

⭕ Trace. ▪ Match. ✏ Color.

The children trace the words with colored pencils.
Then they match the sentences with the corresponding
pictures. Finally, the children color the pictures freely.

I wake up every day.

I get dressed every day.

I wash my face every day.

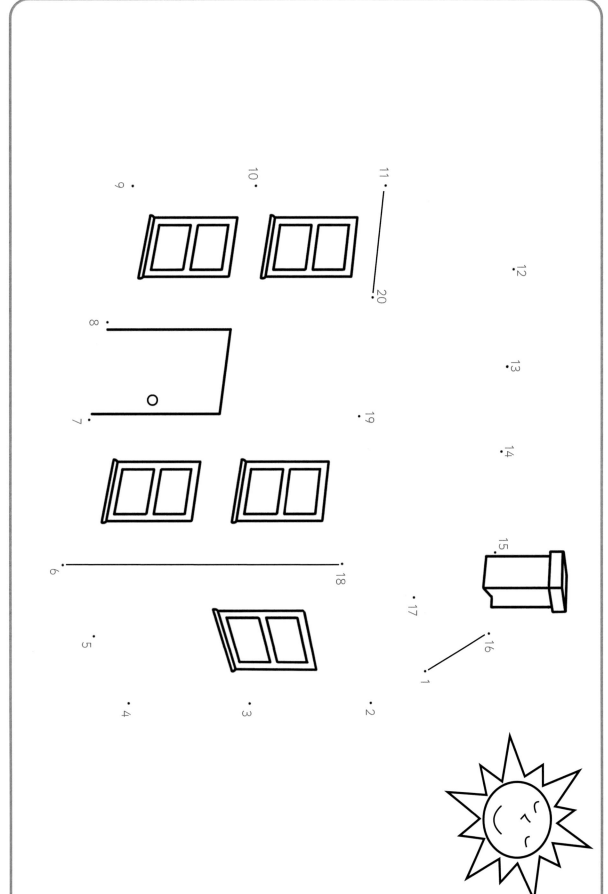

👆 Count. ⬛ Match. ✏️ Color.

Review the numbers from 1 to 20. Then the children count the dots on each bed. Next, they draw lines to match the dots on the beds with the corresponding numbers. Finally, the children color the pictures freely.

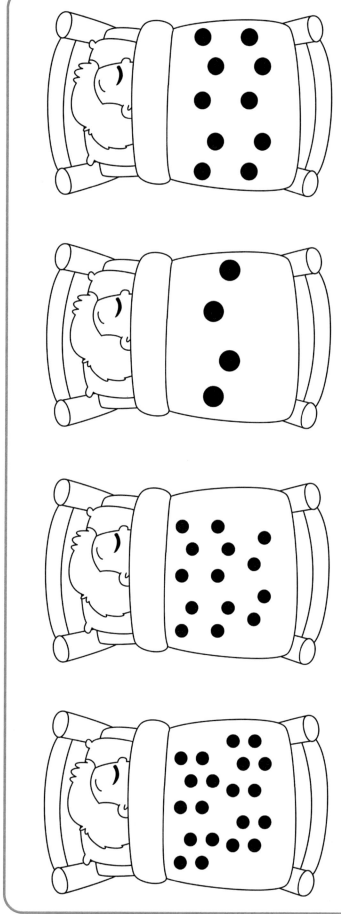

My numbers

✋ Count. ✏ Write.

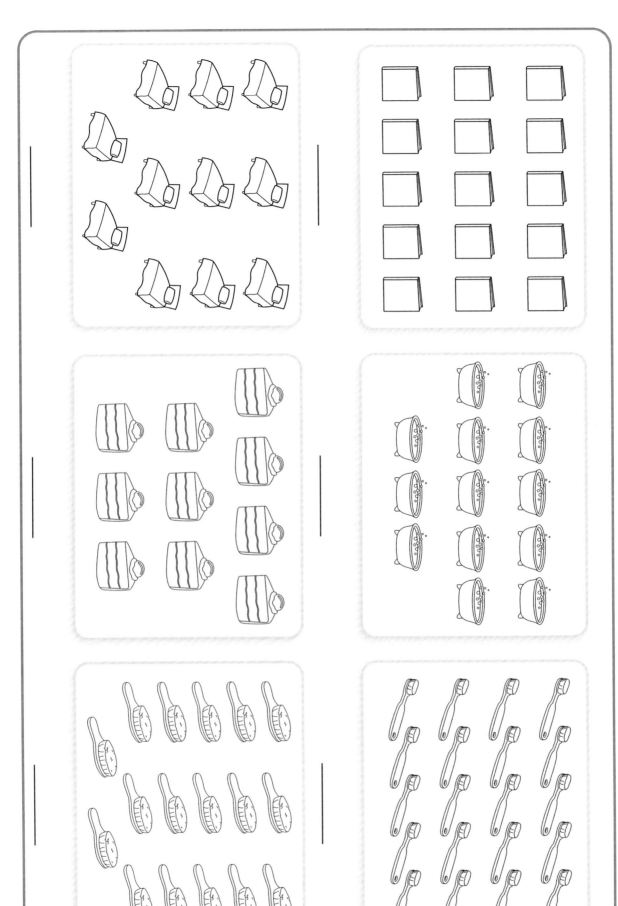

Review the numbers from 10 to 20. Then the children count the objects in each box and write the corresponding number on the lines.

Match. ○ Trace. ✎ Color.

The children trace over each path with a red crayon. Then they trace the corresponding words with colored pencils. Finally, the children color the pictures.

bed

box

lamp

rug

basket

bookcase

14   My letters

○ Trace. Match. Color.

It's next to the cabinet

It's on the bed

It's in the toy box

The children trace the words with colored pencils. Then they draw lines to match the sentences with the corresponding pictures. Finally, the children color the pictures freely.

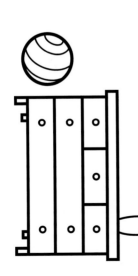

My letters 15

○ **Trace.** ○ **Circle.**

 The children trace the words with colored pencils. Then they circle the correct pictures.

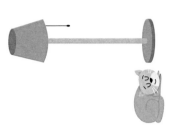

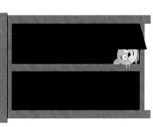

It's under the rug.

It's on the bookcase.

It's next to the lamp.

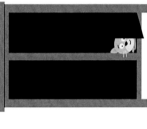

✋ Count. ✏ Color.

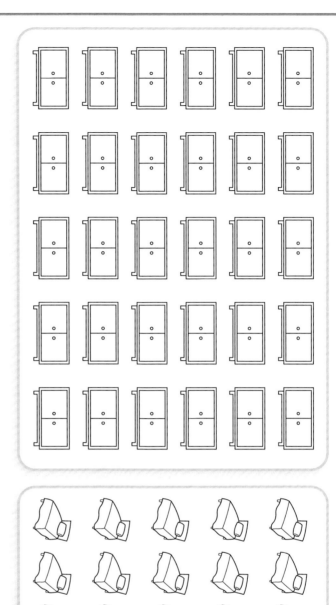

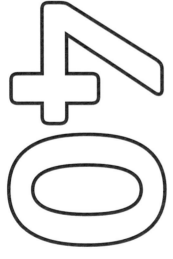

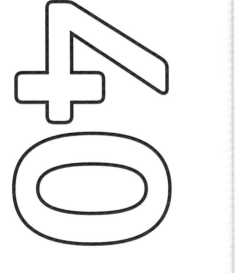

Present the numbers. Then the children count the beds and cabinets in each box. Finally, they color the numbers freely.

30

40

🖐 Count. ⭕ circle.

The children count the objects in each box. Then they circle the corresponding number.

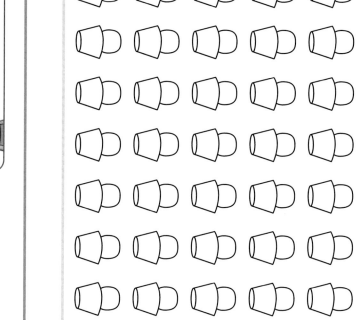

30 40

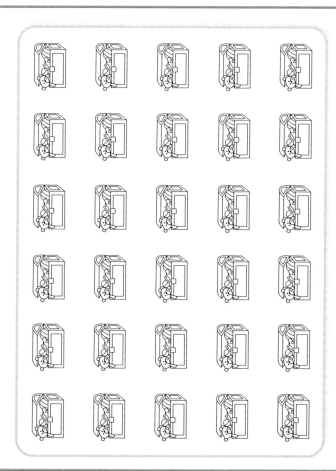

30 40

Count. Draw.

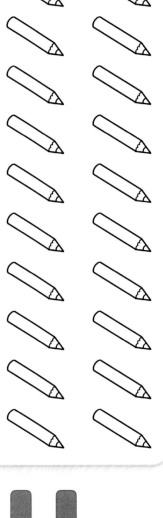

The children count the objects in each box. Then they draw five more of each object to show the correct number.

$\square\square = 40$

$\square\square = 30$

✏ Write. ✏ Color.

The children write the words in the boxes under the correct sport. Then they color the pictures freely.

| badminton | baseball | basketball |
| field hockey | soccer | tennis |

 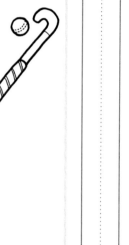 

  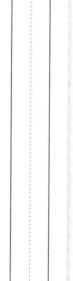

◯ Circle. ✎ Write.

| badminton | basketball |

He's playing

| baseball | tennis |

She's playing

| baseball | soccer |

They're playing

The children circle the corresponding word above each picture. Then they copy the words onto the lines.

○ Circle. ✏ Write.

field hockey

baseball

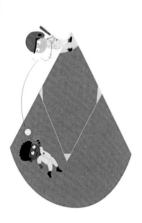

They're playing _____

basketball

soccer

They're playing _____

badminton

tennis

They're playing _____

The children count the balls in each box and match the boxes with the corresponding numbers. Then they color the numbers freely.

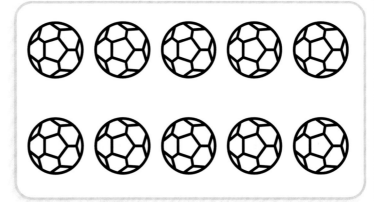

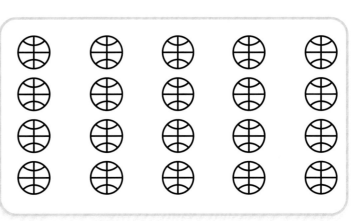

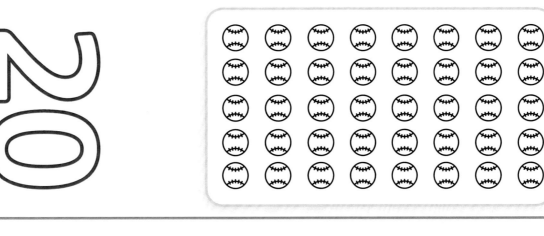

30 40 10 20

✋ Count. ⭕ Trace.

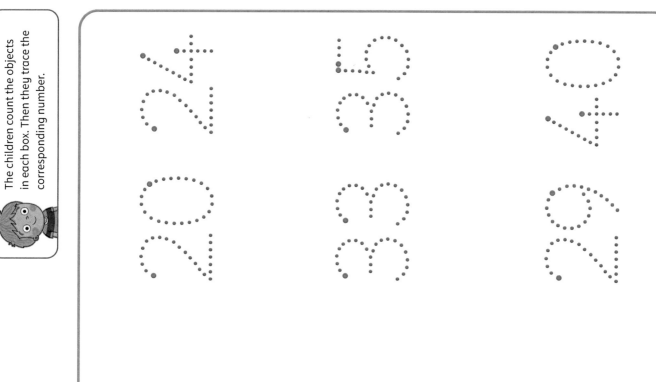

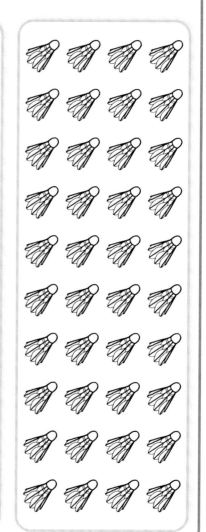

✏ Write. 🖍 Color.

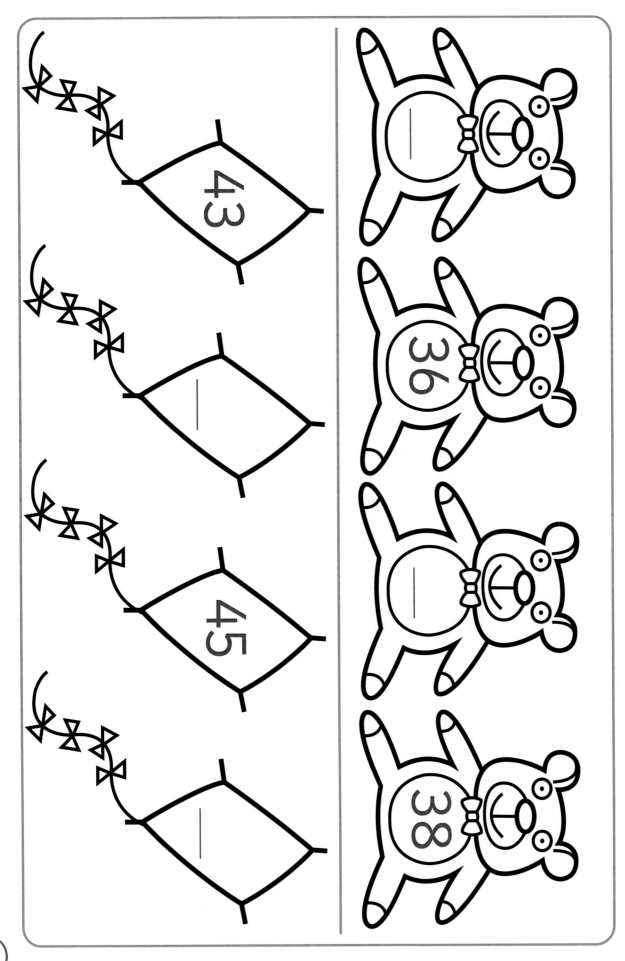

The children complete the two series of numbers. Then they color the pictures freely.

36

38

43

45

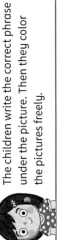

Unit 5

✎ Write. ✐ Color.

The children write the correct phrase under the picture. Then they color the pictures freely.

listening to music

reading books

watching TV

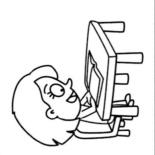

My letters

◯ Trace. ✎ Write. 🖍 Color.

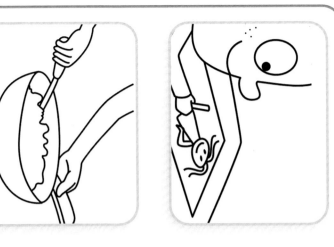

drawing

pictures

cooking

dinner

playing

Video games

The children trace the wavy lines from the pictures to
the words. Then they copy the words onto the lines.
Finally, the children color the pictures freely.

The children copy the words onto the lines to complete each sentence. Then they color the pictures freely.

✏ Write. 🖍 Color.

We like
_____

reading books

I like
_____

watching TV

I like
_____

drawing pictures

🖐 **Count.** ⬭ **Trace.** ✏ **Color.**

Present the number 50. The children count the petals on each flower and trace the numbers. Finally they color the flowers freely.

My numbers **29**

✋ Count. ✏ Color.

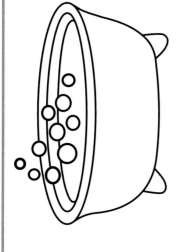
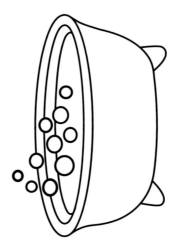

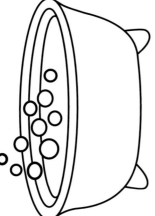
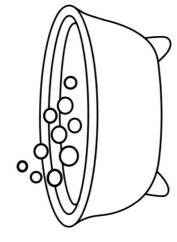

60

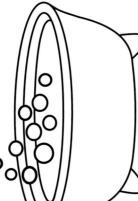
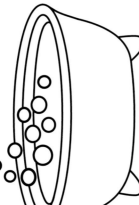
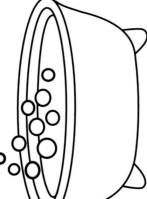
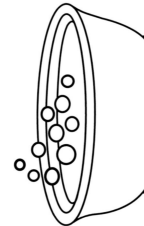

Count. ○ Circle.

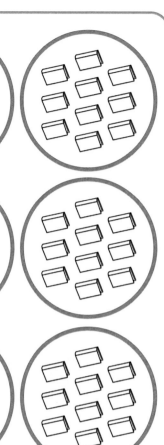

= 55   53   60

= 58   60   57

The children count the books and circle the correct number. Repeat the procedure for the musical notes.

The children trace the words and write a check next to the correct pictures.

Unit 6

○ Trace. ✔ Write a check.

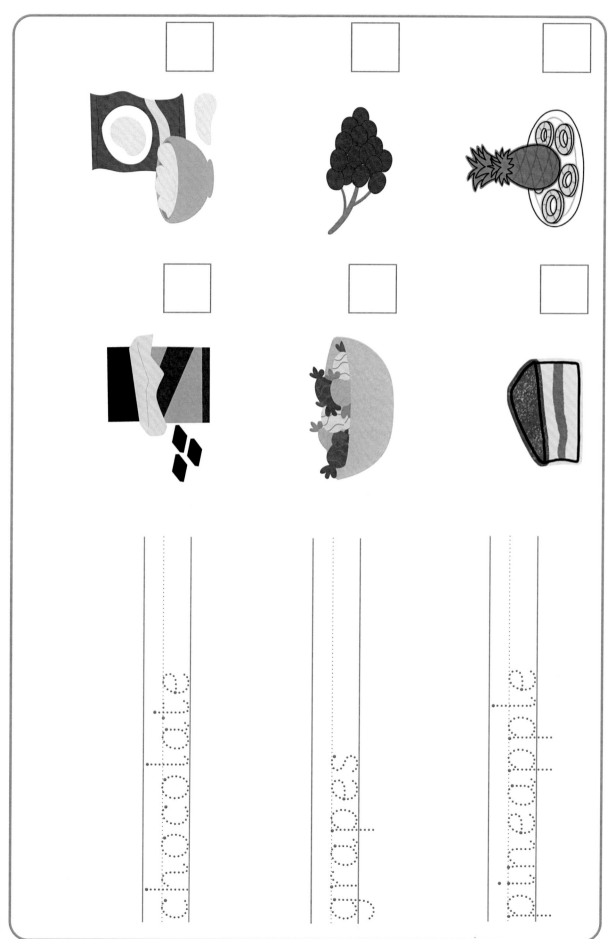

chocolate

grapes

pineapple

32 My letters

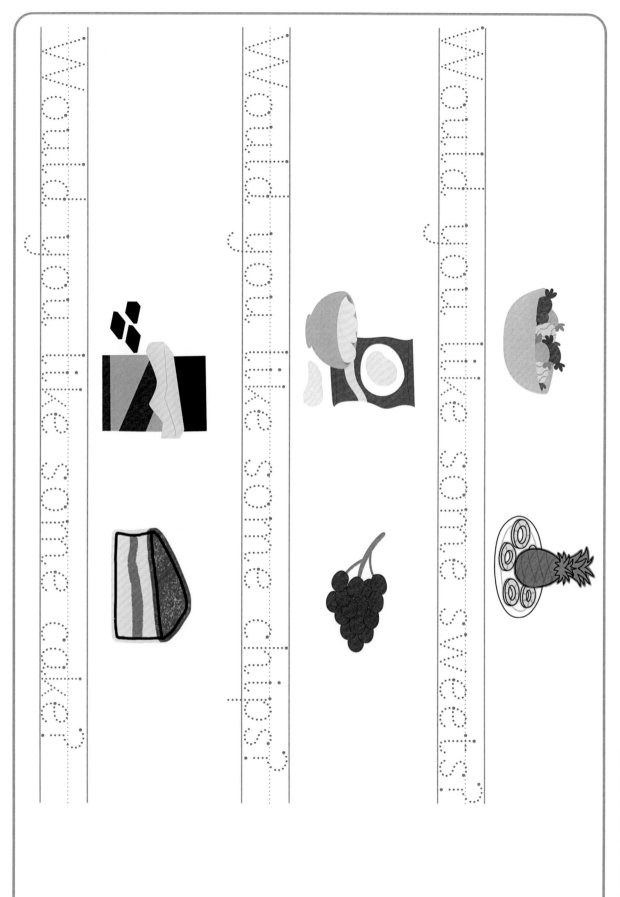

Trace. ○ Circle.

Would you like some cake?

Would you like some chips?

Would you like some sweets?

The children trace the sentences and circle the corresponding pictures.

My letters (33)

The children trace the sentences.
Then the children draw lines to match the sentences to the correct pictures.

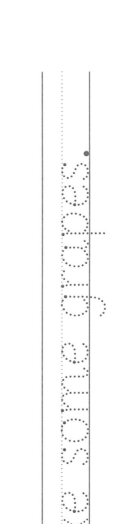

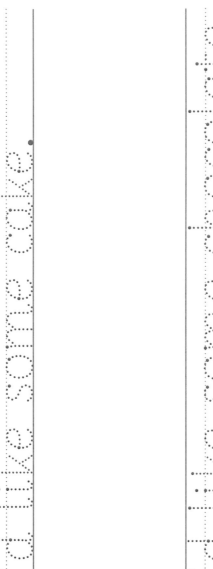

I like some cake

I like some chocolate

I like some grapes

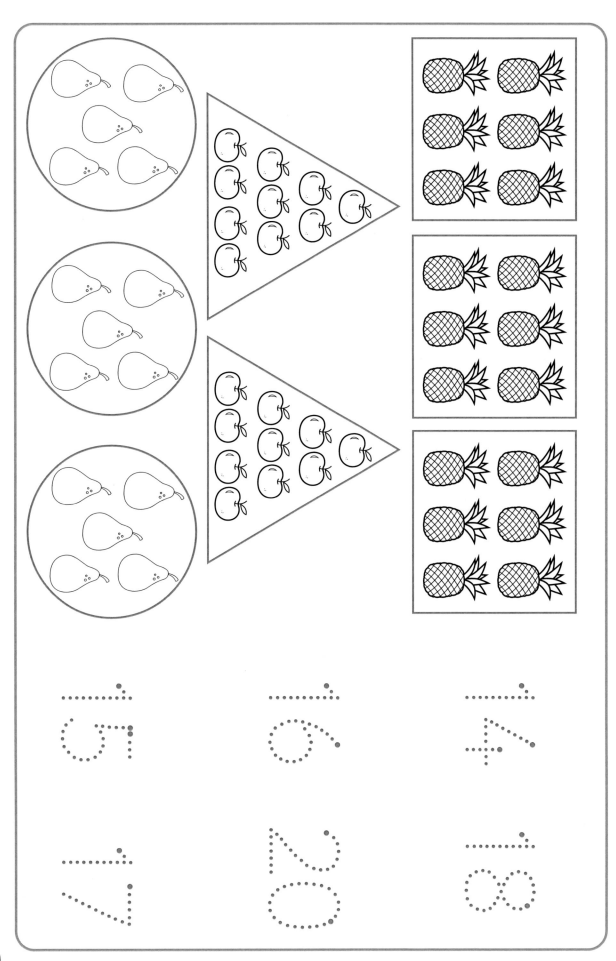

Count. ◯ Trace. ✏ Color.

The children identify and count the pineapples. Then they trace the number that corresponds to the total number of pineapples. Repeat the same procedure for the remaining food items. Finally, the children color the pictures freely.

My numbers (35)

The children count the food items in each box. Then they write the corresponding number next to each picture. Finally, the children color the pictures freely.

✋ Count. ✏ Write. 🖍 Color.

How many?

 _____

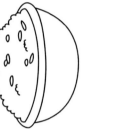 _____

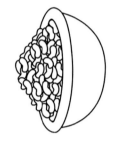 _____

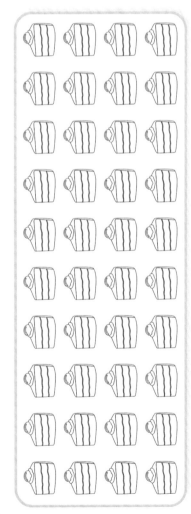

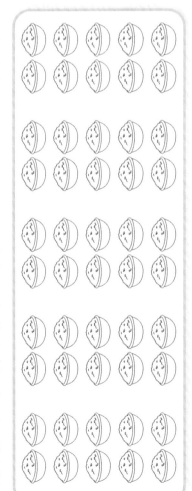

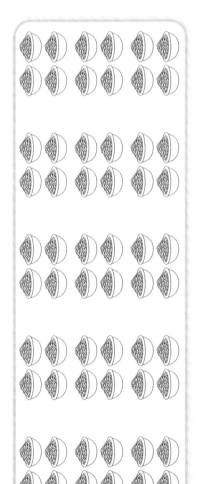

My numbers

✏️ **Write.** 🖍️ **Color.**

Review the numbers from 10 to 80. Then the children look at the picture and write the missing numbers. Finally, they color the picture freely.

10

40

80

Unit 7

The children trace the sentences. Then they draw and color the animals' missing body parts. Finally, the children color the animals freely.

◯ Trace. 🖊 Draw. 🖍 Color.

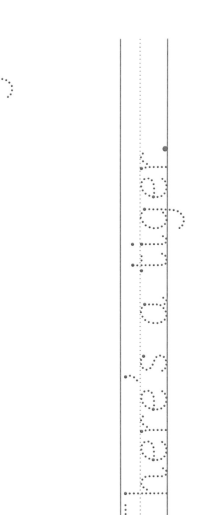

There's a monkey.

There's a tiger.

There's a snake.

Trace. Count. Circle.

There are two elephants

There are three hippos

There are four crocodiles

The children trace the sentences with colored pencils. Then they circle the correct number of elephants, hippos and crocodiles.

○ Trace.  Draw.

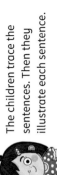

The children trace the sentences. Then they illustrate each sentence.

there's a snake

there are two elephants

there are four elephants

Present the number 70. Next, the children count the sheep in tens. Finally, the children paint the number 70. Alternatively, they can color the number with crayons.

👋 Count. ✏️ Color.

Present the number 80. Then the children count the dots on the butterflies in tens. Finally, they color the dots on each butterfly freely.

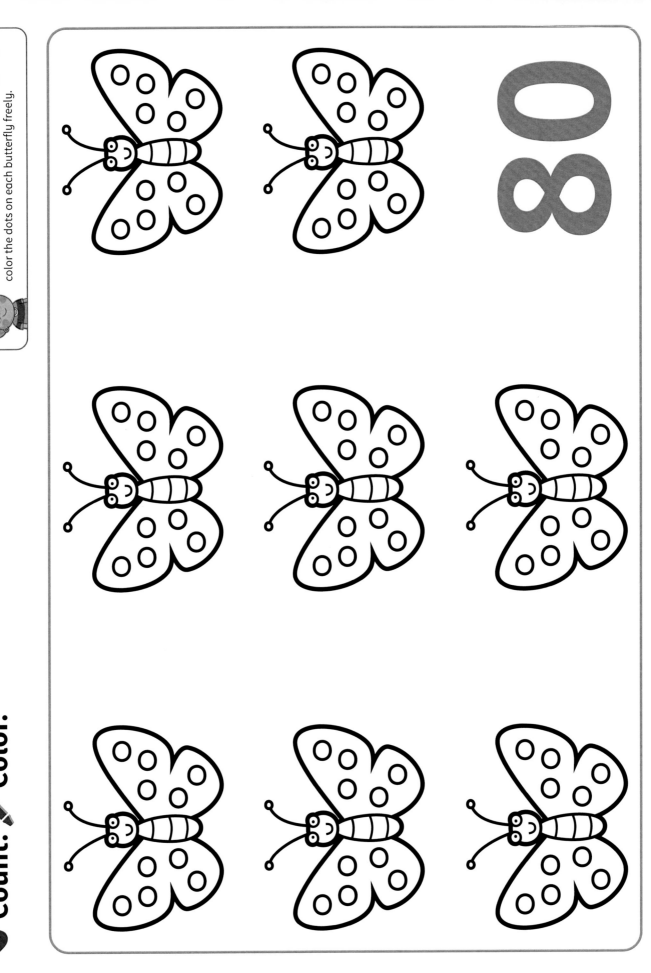

Follow. ✏️ Draw. 🖍️ Color.

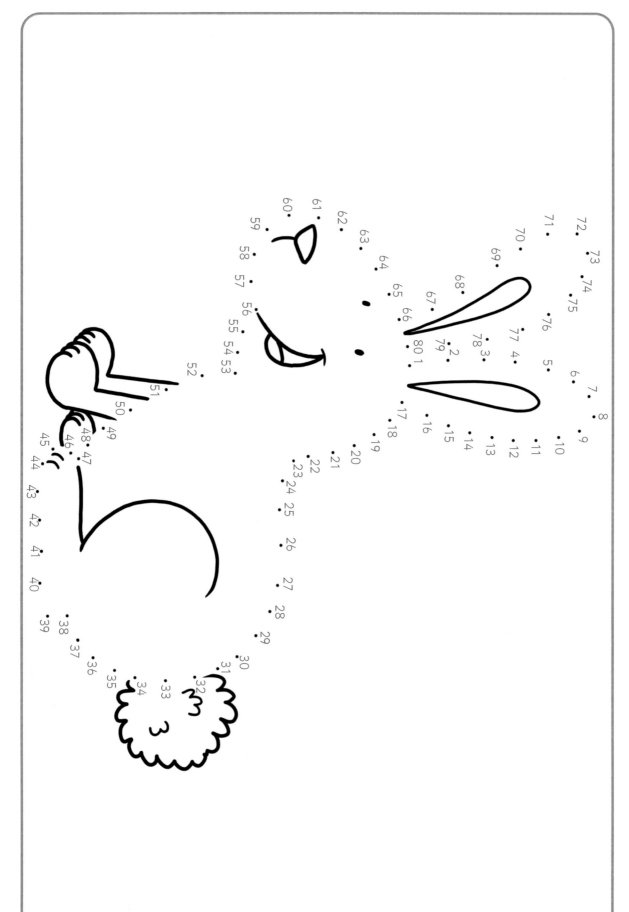

📖 Read. ✏️ Write. ✏️ Color.

The children copy the sentences onto the lines. Then they color the pictures freely.

Plants need rain.

Plants

Plants need soil.

Plants need sun.

Read. ⭕ Circle. ✏️ Write.

The children read the sentences and circle the correct pictures. Then they copy the sentences onto the lines.

What beautiful flowers!

What an old hat!

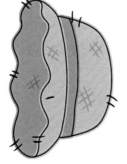

What

Read. ✔ Write a check. ✏ Write.

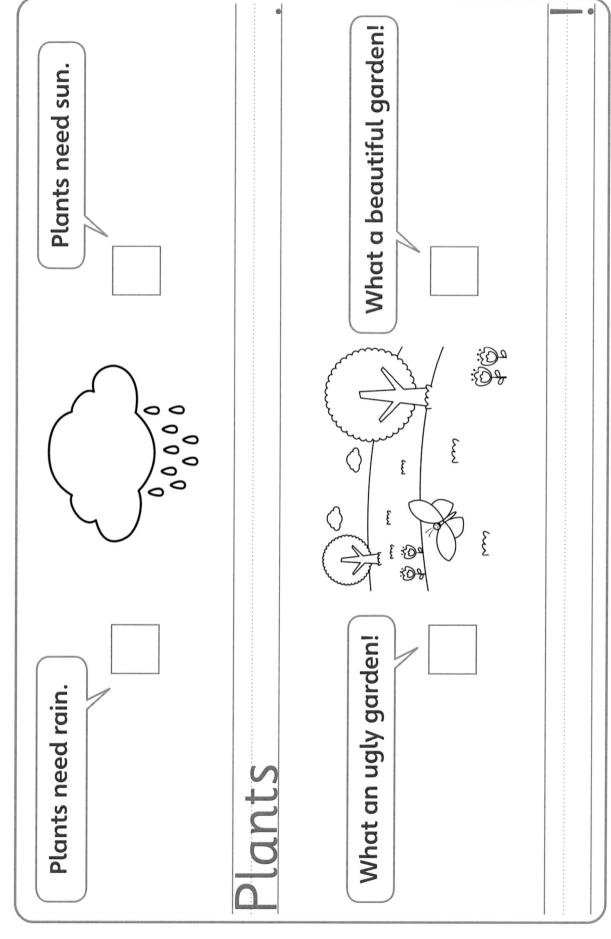

Plants need sun.

Plants need rain.

Plants

What a beautiful garden!

What an ugly garden!

Present the number 90. Then the children count the trees in sets of ten. Finally, they color the number 90.

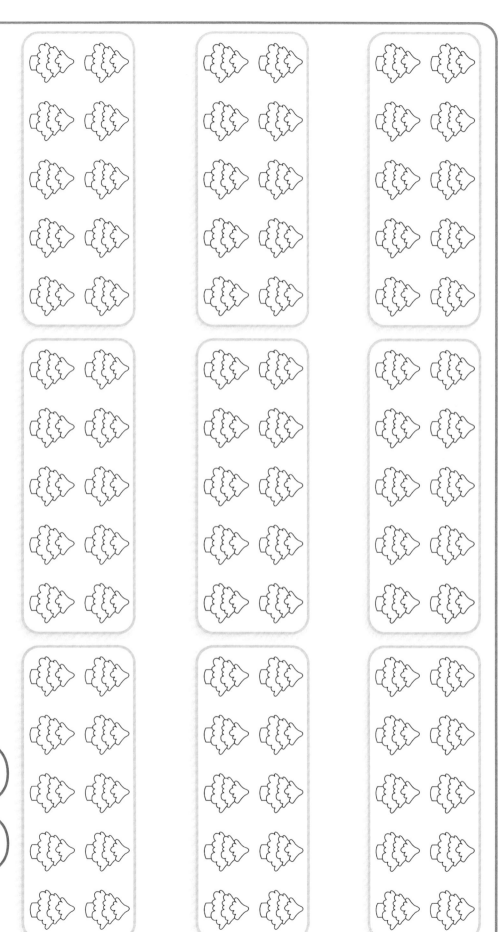

90

✋ Count. ✏ Color.

Present the number 100. The children count the suns in sets of ten. Then they color the number 100 freely.

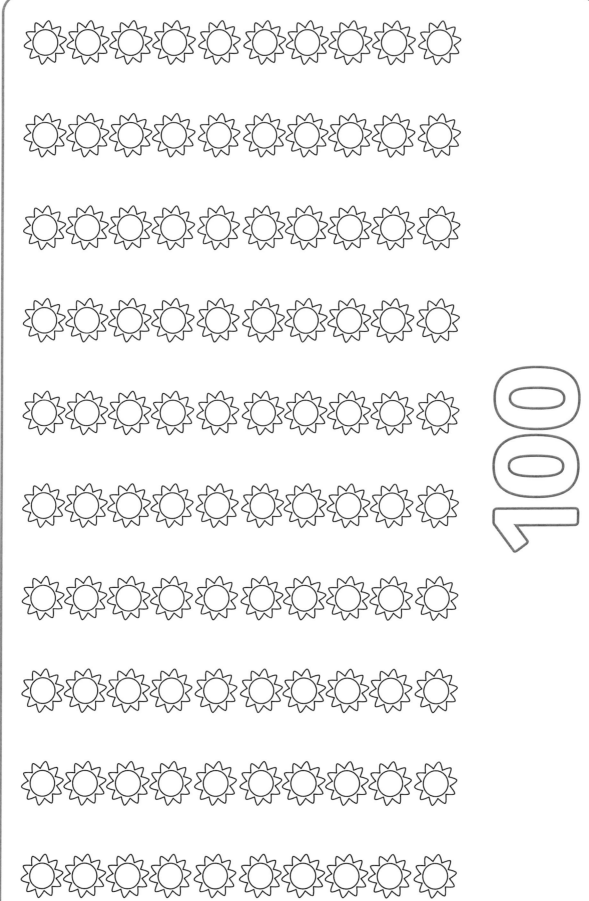

✋ Count. ◯ Circle.

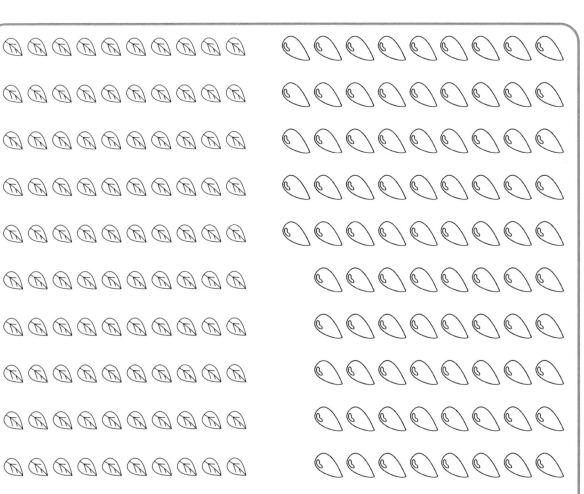

How many?

85   90   93

90   95   100

📖 Read. ✏️ Write. ✏️ Color.

The children complete the sentence with the words *to the supermarket.*
Repeat the procedure for the remaining items. Finally, they color the pictures freely.

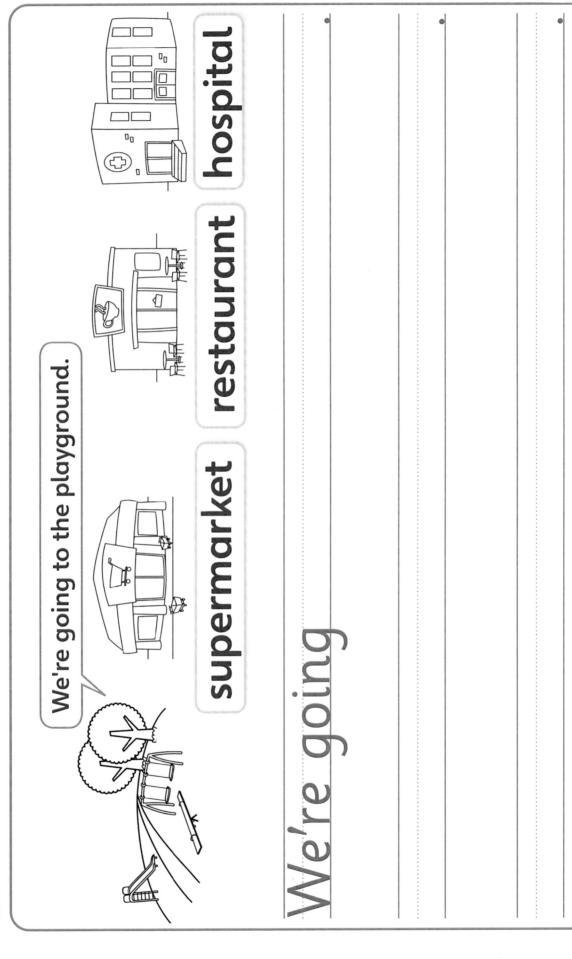

We're going to the playground.

supermarket

restaurant

hospital

We're going

Read. ✏ Write. ✏ Color.

The children read the sentence. Then they copy the words *works in a ...* and complete the sentence with the word *store*. Repeat the procedure for the remaining sentences. Finally, the children color the pictures freely.

A teacher works in a school.

A sales clerk

| sales clerk | store |

doctor

hospital

waiter

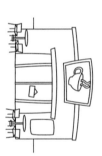

restaurant

✏ Write. 🖍 Color.

I'm going → to → the playground.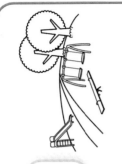

I'm going

We're going → to → the store.

We're going → to → the restaurant.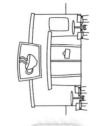

Write. Color.

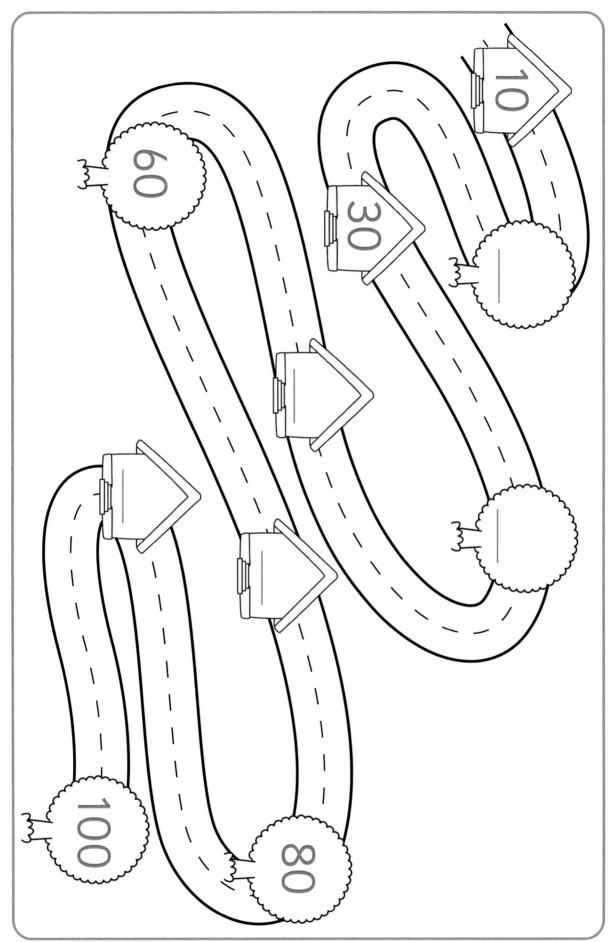

Review the numbers from 10 to 100. Then the children write the missing numbers on the path with colored pencils. Finally, they color the picture freely.

My numbers

(53)

Review the numbers from 10 to 100. Then the children identify the number 10, draw a line from the number 10 to the number 20, and so on, using a colored pencil. Finally, they color the numbers freely.

✏️ Draw. 🖍️ Color.

80

90

70

60

100

20

50

10

30

40

Count. ✗ Cross out.

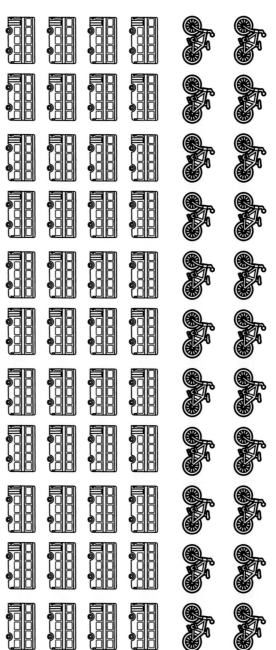

20

43

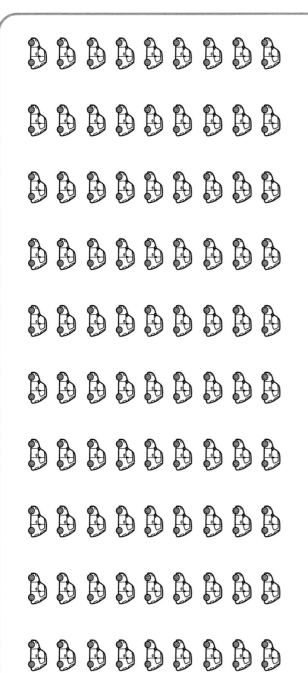

87

Thanks and acknowledgements

The publishers and authors would like to thank the following contributors:

Page makeup by Blooberry Design and QBS Learning.
Cover concept by Blooberry Design. Front cover photography by
NYS444/iStock/Getty Images

Illustrations by Louise Gardner, Marek Jagucki, Sue King (Plum Pudding), and
Bernice Lum. Icons (color, count, draw, look, match, say, trace, tick, write) by
https://thenounproject.com/icon.